# PC Gaming:
## Beginner's Guide

Century Skills **INNOVATION LIBRARY**

Josh Gregory

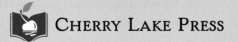
**CHERRY LAKE PRESS**

Published in the United States of America by Cherry Lake Publishing Group
Ann Arbor, Michigan
www.cherrylakepublishing.com

Reading Adviser: Beth Walker Gambro, MS, Ed., Reading Consultant, Yorkville, IL

Library of Congress Cataloging-in-Publication Data

Names: Gregory, Josh, author.
Title: PC gaming : beginner's guide / beginner's guide / by Josh Gregory.
Other titles: Personal computer gaming
Description: Ann Arbor, Michigan : Cherry Lake Publishing, 2022. | Series:
   21st century skills innovation library | Includes bibliographical
   references and index. | Audience: Grades 4-6 | Summary: "By building
   their own custom PCs, video game fans can tweak every detail to make
   sure they get the best possible experience every time they play. In this
   book, readers will learn what makes PC gaming different from other kinds
   of gaming and find out how to get started playing PC games. Includes
   table of contents, author biography, sidebars, glossary, index, and
   informative backmatter"— Provided by publisher.
Identifiers: LCCN 2021042781 (print) | LCCN 2021042782 (ebook) | ISBN
   9781534199682 (library binding) | ISBN 9781668900826 (paperback) | ISBN
   9781668902264 (ebook) | ISBN 9781668906583 (pdf)
Subjects: LCSH: Computer games—Juvenile literature.
Classification: LCC GV1469.15 .G449 2022  (print) | LCC GV1469.15  (ebook)
   | DDC 784.8—dc23
LC record available at https://lccn.loc.gov/2021042781
LC ebook record available at https://lccn.loc.gov/2021042782

Cherry Lake Publishing Group would like to acknowledge the work of the Partnership for 21st Century Learning, a Network of Battelle for Kids. Please visit http://www.battelleforkids.org/networks/p21 for more information.

Printed in the United States of America
Corporate Graphics

**Josh Gregory** is the author of more than 125 books for kids. He has written about everything from animals to technology to history. A graduate of the University of Missouri–Columbia, he currently lives in Chicago, Illinois.

# Contents

# CHAPTER 1

# A Better Way to Play

Today, video games are more popular than they've ever been before. Once considered an expensive hobby for only the most dedicated fans, they have grown to become one of the world's most common forms of entertainment. From dedicated game consoles to cell phones and other mobile devices, there are countless ways to play. But for decades, the most serious game fans have always tended to flock toward one particular method of playing: the personal computer, or PC.

A PC can offer a fully customizable gaming experience. It can do everything the latest gaming consoles can do, plus much more. Are you the type of player who wants the most advanced graphics possible? Do you like your games to run smoothly, at a high **frame rate**? A powerful PC can outperform any other gaming system. PC gaming isn't always about having the latest cutting-edge technology, though. It is also a great way to play older games that aren't available on current consoles. Each person can set up their PC however they want to and focus on any kinds of games that appeal to them.

Playing games on a PC is not always as simple or straightforward as it is on a console or a mobile device. Sometimes it can take a lot of work to keep your computer working smoothly, or to get a certain game to run correctly. If all you want to do is play games, this

When you just want to sit down and enjoy some games with friends or family, consoles are usually your best bet.

## An All-in-One Tool

A PC is a lot more than just a gaming system. You can use it to do almost anything you can think of! Want to watch movies, listen to music, or just surf the internet? You can do all of that and much more, possibly at the same time you are playing a game. If you have a project due for school, you can go online to do research, then type up your findings. Are you a creative person? Use your PC to make art, record music, or edit videos. Are you more interested in technology? Use your PC to practice coding and design your own apps. There is truly no limit to what you can do with your computer as long as you are willing to put in the time and effort to learn new skills as you go.

kind of thing might be frustrating. But for many PC gamers, it is all part of the fun. If you like to tinker with technology, PC gaming could be the perfect hobby for you. Some PC gamers spend more time and energy building and **upgrading** their systems than they spend actually playing games!

If you are new to PC gaming, you might be overwhelmed at first. There is a lot to learn, and some of it might seem very technical. But little by little, it will all start to make sense once you dive in. You might also be surprised to find that the things you learn as a PC gamer can help you in other parts of your life. For example, you're likely

PC gaming is a hobby that's about way more than just playing video games.

to learn a lot about how computers work and what each piece of **hardware** in your machine does. You'll probably also learn a thing or two about electricity and circuits. If you decide to pursue a career in engineering or technology, this knowledge could really come in handy.

If you are interested in PC gaming at all, you have probably spent some time on YouTube watching people showing off their incredible machines and explaining how they were built. At first, you might think that you'll never be as knowledgeable as these experts. But remember that even the most popular PC gamers online started out as beginners. They spent time researching, watching **tutorial** videos, experimenting, and making mistakes. Believe it or not, they are probably still doing most of those things!

At first, the inside of a computer might seem intimidating, but it won't take you long to learn what everything does.

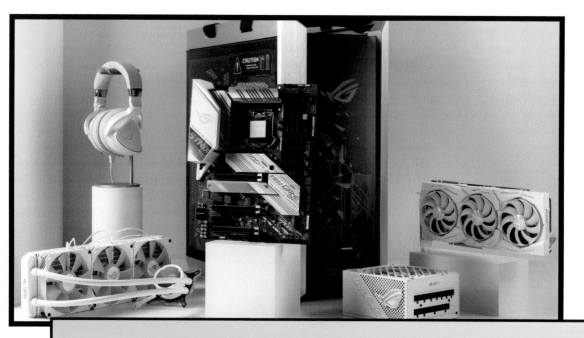

Some PC fanatics are so particular about their parts that they try to match the colors of all their hardware.

Experts always have more to learn when it comes to PC building and gaming. Technology is always expanding and changing, and keeping up with the latest advances can be a full-time job. And with every new technological advance comes a world of new possibilities. PC gamers are known for pushing their machines to the limits and using computers in creative ways.

# CHAPTER 2

# Something for Everyone

For many people, the most appealing part of PC gaming is putting together a fully customized machine. You can choose every individual part on a custom PC, from the video card that powers your games' graphics to the outer case of the machine.

Many people also like to dive in and assemble everything themselves. You don't have to do this if you don't want to. There are many companies that give customers the chance to pick out a selection of computer parts and let a professional handle the assembly. But if you like to build things, you might find a lot of satisfaction in putting your own computer together. You will get a better understanding of how everything works. This will come in handy when you need to do repairs or upgrades in the future. Building your own PC also allows you to shop around for parts.

If you are good at hunting down bargains, this can be a great way to save money.

Building a new PC from scratch can be very expensive. This is especially true if you want to use the latest, most powerful parts available. The good news is that an incredibly powerful computer isn't necessary to enjoy most games. For about the same price as a video game console, it's possible to build a PC that can handle the latest games just fine.

You don't need the fanciest computer available to enjoy popular games like *Roblox*.

Want to poke around and learn about PC hardware without investing hundreds of dollars? Ask relatives if they have an old PC lying around. Or try looking around at thrift stores and secondhand stores. People are always getting rid of older computers when they upgrade to newer technology. Your own family might even have one stashed away in the garage or the basement.

No matter what kind of computer you end up with, you'll be able to have fun with it. You just need to find the right games for your machine. To do this, the first thing you'll need to do is learn your PC's **specs**. These are the basic measurements of your PC's ability to run games. There are a few major ones you'll need to get familiar with. The first is your **processor** speed. The processor is also known as the central processing unit (CPU). Think of a processor as the main piece that allows your computer to "think."

The next spec to consider is how much **memory** your PC has. Memory is handled by random access memory (RAM) chips. The more RAM you have, the more information can be stored in your computer for immediate use. Imagine you were writing a report for school. If you can memorize a lot of facts at once, you can write more before you need to look something up. That's kind of how RAM works. When you are running a game, your computer will load the necessary information into the RAM. More RAM is needed for more complex games.

Hard drive space is a very simple spec. It is simply a measurement of how much storage space you have

# *Mac Gaming*

**Most PC gaming is done on Microsoft Windows. If are building a gaming PC or shopping for one, you should definitely choose a Windows-based machine. But maybe the only computer your family has at home is a Mac. Don't worry. You can still use it to play games!**

**Most regular PC games will not run on a Mac. Instead, you'll need special Mac versions. Other than that, running games on a Mac is a lot like running them on a Windows PC. You'll have to make sure your Mac meets the minimum system requirements. Then you can tweak the game's settings to get it running how you like it. The biggest difference between Windows PC gaming and Mac gaming is that you can't really build a custom Mac machine. You can choose from a few options when you buy a Mac, but not nearly as many as you can when you put together a Windows machine.**

available for files on your computer. A bigger hard drive means you can install more games at once. Hard drives can also have different speeds. This can affect how long it takes for your computer to load games.

Finally, when it comes to gaming, you'll often have to pay close attention to the speed of your video card. This is the device that generates the graphics you see on screen while playing a game. It is often the most expensive part in a gaming PC. The most advanced video cards can costs thousands of dollars all on their

A video card can make or break your PC's ability to run the latest games.

own! But as with all things PC gaming, there are always much more affordable options that work just fine.

If you built your own machine, you'll probably already have a pretty good idea of your specs from the time you spent comparing and shopping for parts. If you are playing on a machine someone else built or on an older PC, you might have to poke around a little to find the information you need. For example, in Windows 10 you can right-click the Start menu and select System from the menu that appears. This will let you quickly check your processor and RAM. Finding out what kind of video card you have or how much hard drive space you have could require digging through some other menus. And you are using an **operating system** other than Windows 10, the process will be completely different. This might seem frustrating. But don't forget, experimenting and learning are big parts of PC gaming!

Every PC game has a set of system requirements. If you are buying a hard copy of the game, the requirements will be printed on the box. If you are buying a digital copy, the requirements will likely be listed on the game's download page. Most of the time, you will see two sets of requirements. The first is the list of minimum requirements. These are the very lowest specs that are still able to run the game. The other set of requirements is the recommended set. These specs are what you'll need to run the game the way its **developers** think is best for enjoying the experience.

One of the simplest upgrades you can make is to add more RAM to your computer.

System requirements are just a general guide. Remember that PC gaming is all about doing things your own way. Pretty much every game allows you to adjust all kinds of settings for its graphics and other features. This means you might be able to turn down the settings to make a game run on a slower computer. Or if you have a really powerful computer, you can crank the game's settings up and push your machine to the limits!

The number of different possible combinations of parts in a gaming PC is nearly limitless. Developers do their best to make sure their games will run on as many computers as possible. But they can't test every possible combination of different specs and settings. This means you might eventually have issues running a game even though your machine seems to meet the minimum requirements. Usually, these kinds of problems can be solved by adjusting some settings or updating a piece of **software**. Other times, you might need to wait for the developers to release a game update that solves the issue. Either way, consider going online to see if others are having the same issue. This is often the fastest way to find a solution!

# CHAPTER 3

# The Perfect Setup

There is a lot more to PC gaming than just the PC itself. You'll need a screen to play on, a way to control your games, and much more. The good news is that there are just as many ways to customize these options as there are to customize your actual PC.

One thing you'll definitely need is some kind of monitor. Choosing a monitor for your PC is a lot like shopping for a new TV. First, you'll need to think about what size and shape you want your screen to be. Some computer monitors are about the same shape as a standard TV screen. Others are incredibly wide. Some are quite small, while others are massive. Many serious PC gamers hooks up multiple monitors at once. Having two screens next to each other is a fairly common setup. This lets players enjoy a game on one screen while chatting with friends or surfing the internet on the other. For some people, even two screens isn't enough. They might hook up three or even more at a time!

Choosing the right monitor is more than just finding one that's the right size. You also need to look at different screens to see how bright they are and how they display colors. Different monitors can also display different **resolutions**. A screen with a higher resolution can display a more detailed image. Be careful though.

An ultrawide monitor like this one lets you see more of the action at once when you're playing a game.

Running modern games at very high resolutions often requires a very powerful PC.

You'll also need to decide how you want to set up your PC's audio system. Many people like wearing headphones while they play. A good set of headphones can make it feel like you are really in the game. They

Many PC gamers like to wear headphones with built-in microphones so they can talk to teammates and friends as they play.

A good set of speakers can make games, movies, and music more enjoyable. Just make sure you aren't bothering anyone when you turn them up!

are also useful if you want to play around other people who might be bothered by the sound.

Some people prefer to use speakers. This could mean anything from a small set of speakers that fits on a desk to a full surround-sound stereo setup with speakers mounted around the room. Don't forget that you can use your gaming PC to watch movies and listen to music. If you spend a lot of time doing these things, you might want a really good sound system.

You'll also need some way to control the action when you're playing. The most basic way to control a PC game is to use a mouse and keyboard. You will likely have these things anyway, since you need them to set

## PC Gaming on the Go

Do you travel a lot? Do you like to bring your games over to your friends' houses to play? Moving a full-size gaming PC around can be a real pain once you've set it up. Your setup might have a bunch of different parts, with all kinds of cables connecting them. Plus, things like monitors must be handled carefully so you don't damage them.

The solution if you want to bring your PC games on the go is simple: use a laptop! Laptops used to struggle with modern games. They simply weren't powerful enough. But today's laptop technology is much better at keeping up with the latest games. Unlike a regular desktop PC, you probably won't build your own laptop. However, pretty much everything else works exactly the same. You can even hook up a laptop to a big monitor and game controller when you are at your desk.

up the PC and use it for everyday tasks. Even these seemingly simple devices can be customized, though! Some players have very specific preferences for how they want the keys on their keyboards to feel, or what shape their mouse should be.

In addition to the standard mouse and keyboard, you might want a regular gamepad like the ones you would use with a video game console. In fact, you can even use PlayStation and Xbox controllers to play most PC games if you like. There are also all kinds of other controllers out there to choose from, so feel free to find one that works best for you.

If you play certain types of games a lot, you might even want a special controller for them. For example, some players really love games that let them fly airplanes and spaceships. They put together large, multipart controllers that make it feel like they are really in the cockpits of these flying vehicles. Racing game fans often use steering wheels and pedals to control the action. Serious fighting game players use arcade-style fight sticks. Many of them even build their own fight sticks from scratch. They choose the shape and feeling of each button and assemble everything on their own.

You're probably going to be spending a lot of time at your desk, so it's good to create an environment you enjoy.

Of course, you'll also need somewhere to set up all this equipment. For most people, this means setting up a computer desk. You'll want to make sure your desk has enough room to comfortably hold your monitor, keyboard, mouse, and any other equipment. You'll also want a comfortable chair that allows you to sit up straight while you play.

Some PC gamers take their desk setups very seriously. They might set up lights that change to match the colors on screen during a game. Or they might make sure everything from their chair to their keyboard has a matching look. Some people also find creative ways to hide the many cables and wires on their PCs.

If you prefer, you can hook your gaming PC up to a regular TV and play that way instead. To do this, you'll probably need a wireless keyboard, mouse, and game controller. Otherwise, hooking a modern PC up to a TV isn't much different than plugging in a game console.

# CHAPTER 4

# Play Time

Once you've got a PC gaming setup put together, it's time for the really fun part: actually playing games! One of the great things about PC gaming is that there are many, many ways to get games. If you shop around, you can usually find deals and save a lot of money compared to what you might pay to play on a video game console. You can even find a lot of great games that are given away completely free! Even if your gaming budget is low, you'll never run out of things to play on a gaming PC.

Most PC games are sold through digital stores such as Steam and the Epic Games store. For each of these services, you'll download an app to your PC and make an account. Then, when you purchase games, they will be linked to your account. You can download them through the app. You can also take advantage of the app's features to download updates for your games, stay up to date with gaming news, and more.

If you have an older PC, or if you just like playing classic games, check out the GOG digital store. This store specializes in selling older games. Some of them date all the way back to the 1980s and 1990s! These games are often inexpensive, and they are a great way to learn about gaming history. Many classics are still a lot of fun to play today.

You don't need any special equipment to play retro games on a PC.

Another unique place to get games is itch.io. This store specializes in games created by small, independent developers. You probably won't find the latest 3D graphics in these games, but you will find plenty of creativity.

Are you interested in trying lots of games at once? Consider signing up for a subscription service such as

There are hundreds of thousands of games available on itch.io, and many of them are free to play.

Google's Stadia allows players to enjoy games by streaming them instead of downloading or installing them the traditional way.

Microsoft's Game Pass or Google's Stadia Pro. For a monthly fee, these services let you play as many games as you want. The only catch is that you have to keep paying every month if you want to keep playing.

Of course, you can always get PC games the old-fashioned way: by buying discs from stores. If you do this, make sure your computer has a DVD or Blu-Ray drive. Many modern computers do not have these features. And if you really want discs, read the box of a PC game carefully before you buy it. Some boxed games sold at stores don't have anything inside but a code that lets you download the game from a digital store.

There's a lot of information to take in if you are new to PC games. But once you get into it, everything will be second nature. Jump in, and don't be afraid to get creative and try new things. Most importantly, have a great time!

## Careful Communication

One of the most fun parts of PC gaming is sharing the experience with other players. Organizing strategies with teammates over voice chat or sending messages to your friends on Discord are all part of the experience. But remember that you should always be careful when talking to people online. Unless you already know and trust someone in real life, never share any personal information about yourself. And if anyone ever says anything to you that makes you feel uncomfortable, end the conversation right away and tell a trusted adult.

With enough practice, you might even be able to make it as a professional PC gamer one day!

## GLOSSARY

**coding** (KOH-ding) writing instructions for a computer using a programming language

**developers** (dih-VEL-uh-purz) people who make video games or other computer programs

**frame rate** (FRAYM RAYT) a measurement of how many times per second the image on screen changes when playing a game

**hardware** (HARD-wair) the physical parts that make up a computer

**memory** (MEM-uh-ree) a device that is able to hold information for later use

**operating system** (AH-pur-ay-ting SIS-tuhm) a program, such as Microsoft Windows or macOS, that controls the functions of a computer

**processor** (PRAH-sess-ur) the central "brain" of a computer that processes information

**resolutions** (rez-uh-LOO-shuhnz) measurements of how detailed images are

**software** (SAWFT-wair) computer programs

**specs** (SPEKS) details of a computer's abilities

**tutorial** (too-TOR-ee-uhl) a video or web page explaining in detail how to do something

**upgrading** (UP-gray-ding) replacing something with a better version

## FIND OUT MORE

**Books**

Cunningham, Kevin. *Video Game Designer*. Ann Arbor, MI: Cherry Lake Publishing, 2016.

Loh-Hagan, Virginia. *Video Games*. Ann Arbor, MI: Cherry Lake Publishing, 2021.

Powell, Marie. *Asking Questions About Video Games*. Ann Arbor, MI: Cherry Lake Publishing, 2016.

**Websites**

**Logical Increments**
*www.logicalincrements.com/*
This incredibly useful website will help you find parts that work well together and see how much they cost.

**PC Gamer**
*www.pcgamer.com/*
Keep up with the latest PC gaming news.

## INDEX